HOW TO TRIM
WEED FAST

By Sage Liskey
Edited by Jon Cox and Hallie Roberts
Published by the Rad Cat Press

1st Edition

First Edition, November, 2016

Published in the United States by the Rad Cat Press.
Written and designed by Sage Liskey.
Edited by Jon Cox and Hallie Roberts.

Printed in the United States of America
1st Edition

ISBN 9780986246111

www.trimweedfast.com
www.sageliskey.com
www.facebook.com/radcatpress

10% of profits from this publication go to
sustainable reforestation and
old-growth preservation.

TABLE OF CONTENTS

Introduction... 1
Types of Trimming.. 2
Materials... 6
Basics for Trim Bosses and Growers..................... 13
Basics of Trimming Under a Grower or Trim Boss.............. 22
Trim Tightness.. 28
Problems To Look For.. 29
Trimmer Stereotypes.. 30
How To Trim.. 32
Techniques to Trim Fast... 44
Glossary.. 53
Weight and Mass References.................................. 61
About the Author.. 64

Disclaimer!

We do not guarantee the accuracy of the information contained within this guide and expressly disclaim liability for errors and omissions. We further do not guarantee the legality of the techniques discussed and suggest the reader check in with federal, state, county, and city laws prior to using the information contained herein.

INTRODUCTION

Recent medical and recreational legalization of weed has skyrocketed the demand of not just growers of the cannabis plant, but also trimmers to process the flowers of the plants into beautifully shaped nugs. Weed trimming is a lucrative career with many perks. Why trim fast? You'll get paid more at sites that pay you per pound, impress clients, get more jobs, finish processing your personal harvest faster so it will be ready to sell sooner, and be able to teach trimmers you hire how to trim fast.

Trimming takes the heart of a lion, patience of a sloth, and skills of a hawk. This guide introduces common language, materials, basic trimming techniques, advanced trimming techniques, and general guidelines for trimmers, growers, and trim bosses. See the glossary for terminology you may be unfamiliar with.

Note that your state may require special licensing and guidelines in order to legally trim. Please see the disclaimer below the Table of Contents.

TYPES OF TRIMMING

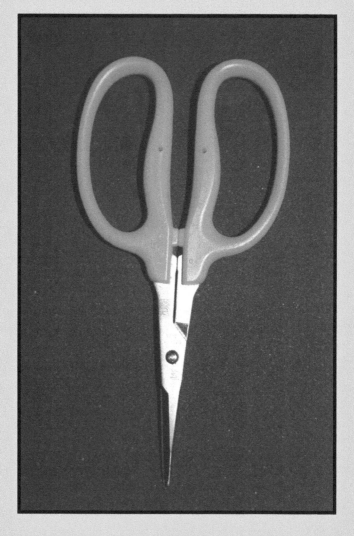

There are several ways to trim weed explained next. Further how-to descriptions will be given in the following sections.

Wet vs. Dry Trimming

Weed may be trimmed immediately after being cut off the living plant and then dried (wet trimming), or dried first and then trimmed (dry trimming). Wet trimming should be done within an hour and a half of cutting plant material down from a plant still in the ground, otherwise the leaves will become flaccid and difficult to trim by hand or machine. Compared to dry trimming, wet weed can be worked with more roughly, dries faster and looks nicer after being trimmed, and in vertical drying systems, such as hanging baskets, requires less space to dry in. Dry trimming removes more trichomes when the weed is touched or dropped but the trimming can be done anytime. Since the branches can be hung with simple hooks and string or wire, the materials required for drying weed to be dry trimmed are also cheaper.

Machine vs. Hand Trimmed

Hand trimmed weed is just like it sounds, you use scissors or your fingers to trim it. Machine trimmers are becoming more and more popular for their speed and thus money saving opportunities, but are

very expensive. While the final product often doesn't look nearly as nice as hand trimmed weed, and the oil used may prevent the trim from being used in certain extracts, many buyers don't care, or the cost savings counterbalance the lower price earned from machine trimmed weed. Some human work is still needed but it is minimal when compared to hand trimming. Spherical nugs do best in trim machines while varieties that have many pits do not run through well. Machine trimming dry weed should be avoided as it makes many of the trichomes and sugar leaf fall off, thus lowering the weed's quality.

Bud Holding vs. Stem Holding

It tends to be easier to trim weed by holding onto the bud itself, but some growers prefer to minimize contact with the buds to prevent trichome loss and ask trimmers to trim while holding onto the stem. If you're asked to do this, you can either leave longer stems on buds or trim while the buds are still on the branch.

Loose vs. Tight Trim

While you're trimming, the trim boss might ask for a looser or tighter trim. More likely though they will tell you that your trimming is too loose and you need to trim tighter; trim bosses almost always want a tighter trim. A tight trim removes all dark green leaves, gets into the nooks and crannies, and shapes the nug into a relatively smooth plane. While trimming loose you keep some smaller leaves, either for aesthetic purposes or because the buyer doesn't care. It is better to

NUGS BUDS WEED GANJA HERB

start off loose when trimming and tighten up after being asked to. Your trimming abilities will generally be more appreciated the tighter you trim, but it does slow you down. Trim bosses may ask you to loosen up your trimming if you are shaving the buds, because at that point you are removing a lot of the trichomes. See the chapter "Trim Tightness" for examples.

A-Bud vs. B-Bud Trimming

B-buds are generally smaller than a dime after being trimmed or are too larfy (airy) to trim without falling apart, though the designation may change depending on the trim boss and the average size of the buds you are trimming. A-buds are buds large enough to trim. See the "How To Trim" chapter for pictures. Most trim bosses will not have you trim B-buds and instead have you separate them into a B-bud bag. These B-buds will either be trimmed later for a higher wage, trimmed through a machine, or processed into a product such as oil. The B-buds must still be individually separated from the branch.

Not Trimming

Some people believe that the trimming process is absurd and enjoy smoking untrimmed weed. However, weed tastes better with the leaves trimmed off, and well-trimmed nugs are essential to obtaining a good price in the increasingly competitive weed industry. You can sometimes find buyers for untrimmed weed, but then that buyer will trim it and make a substantial profit. If your weed is for your personal consumption you might be able to get away with not trimming it, at least until you want to smoke it. Either way you'll still want to buck down the buds from branches (see the "How To Trim" chapter) in order to save space and properly cure your crop (please read other resources for the proper drying and curing of weed).

MATERIALS

Depending on whether you're trimming for yourself or trimming under a trim boss you'll want certain materials to make your job easier. Each item is noted with who should be responsible for supplying it, a (G) for grower/trim boss and/or a (Tr) for trimmer. Be forewarned that trimmers and trim bosses do not always follow these guidelines.

Plastic Bins / Totes (G)

Plastic bins are used for transporting freshly cut down or dried weed branches in. They are also great for temporarily putting stems and trim into as well as maintaining the moisture content of dried weed if the lid is kept on. Bins at least 18 inches wide, 24 inches long, and 18 inches deep are ideal.

Some growers also have trimmers place trimmed buds directly into hard plastic containers with lids, filling them in half-pound increments to be sold directly to dispensaries. These bins can later be picked up and reused. Unlike turkey bags, the plastic shell helps prevent the buds from being crushed or jostled too much.

Scale (G)

The scale weighs out each trimmer's total weed trimmed in grams, or the standard sale amount for growers in the weed market, a pound. Typically large bags of weed cannot fit onto a scale, so a light plastic container or other platform must be used. Don't forget to tare out the weight of the bag containing the weed and the platform holding the bag up. See the back of this guide for weight and mass references.

Gloves (G)

Plastic gloves can be used while working with weed to keep the resin off your fingers. Gloves can make buds harder to handle, so many people only use gloves while big leafing. If your hands get too sweaty, cut away part of the glove to make it more comfortable.

Overhead Lighting (G)

Good lighting allows you to see the nooks and crannies of a bud better!

Music Player (G)

Anything that can pump some jams works, but preferably something with auxiliary cables that plug into smart phones or other portable audio players.

Cooling and Heating Devices (G)

Having a fan or air conditioner is essential to maintain worker happiness and prevent buds from drying out too much, especially in small rooms full of hot trimmers. Alternatively you might need a heater in drafty rooms or later parts of the year.

Tables (G)

You want a table that you can easily rest your hands on while sitting in your chair. Six to eight-foot long folding tables work well, but any surface that you're willing to get covered in resin is fine.

Chairs (G)

Your trimmers will be spending a lot of time in chairs while working, so you want the right kind to maximize their endurance. Stationary and firm chairs that don't move when leaned against are preferable, so avoid purchasing certain types of swivel chairs, camp chairs, or reclining chairs. Chairs with an adjustable height can accommodate different sizes of trimmer, but most trim scenes use simple metal or plastic folding chairs with a little bit of cushion on the seat.

Drop Cloth (G)

Keeps your floor or table clean. A tarp works too.

Cups (G)

Glass or plastic cups for holding the alcohol, oil, and scissors in. Glass is preferable because it has a heavier base and is harder to knock over.

Isopropyl Alcohol (G)

Alcohol is great for removing resin from scissors, especially given a wipe down with a cloth or paper towel after a few minutes of soaking. Trim scenes sometimes only have oil, so it might be a good idea to bring your own alcohol.

Plant-Based Oil (G)

Oil is helpful for keeping resin off of fingers and scissors. Just get a bit on your finger and rub it all over your hands. Towel off any excess afterward. Oil is also useful for scrubbing resin off the hands at the end of the day or during a break. Some say that the best oil to use is coconut oil, but vegetable oil, canola oil, and olive oil also work fine. Trim scenes may only have isopropyl alcohol,

9

so it might be a good idea to bring your own oil. Oil will prevent hash balls from sticking together, and some trim bosses dislike people using oil at all because it can ruin the trichomes in weed if used too heavily. So long as you towel off the excess though, it should not be a problem.

Broom and Dustpan (G)

Trim, stems, and big leaf get everywhere while trimming. Have on hand several brooms and dust pans in order to clean your space periodically or at the end of the day with the help of your trimmers.

Grocery Paper Bags (G)

Paper bags are handy for putting A-buds, B-buds, stems, and trim into. You can go to most grocery stores and buy a stack for cheap.

Turkey Bags (G)

A strong type of plastic oven bag that growers often use for putting A-buds, B-buds, and trim into.

Paper Towels (G)

Used for wiping resin, alcohol, and oil off of scissors and hands. Keep a roll on the table.

Labeling Tools (G)

You'll want paper or tape and a writing tool to label the different varieties of weed, the B-bud bag, the trim bag, as well as each of the trimmer's trimmed bags of weed with the weed variety, weight trimmed, and name of the trimmer. Label everything at the beginning of the trimming session! A notepad with a tally of trimmer's daily weight or hour totals is also essential.

First Aid Supplies (G)

There are always a few snipped fingers so stock some band-aids.

Green Lights (G)

If your trimmers are passing by or interacting with live weed plants at night have green spectrum lights for them to use.

Scissors (G/Tr)

The right pair of scissors will help you trim faster and longer. There are straight, angled, curved, ergonomic, stick resistant, and spring-loaded scissors. You want pruning or gardening scissors with a pointed tip and no friction between the blades, not regular scissors. Different people like different styles, so it is up to you to experiment. Common brands include Chikamasa (bottom right), ARS (top right), and Fiskars (left). Most trim scenes will supply you with scissors, but they tend to be dull and cheap. Buy two or three pairs of your own, mark the handles with a permanent marker, and guard them with your life! It is also recommended that you keep a pair of scissors specifically for cutting through branches and stems while

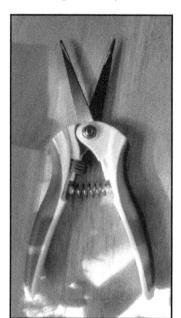
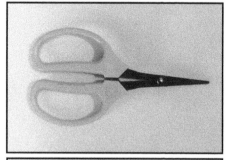
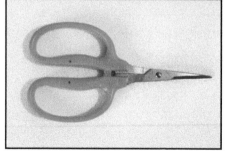

bucking down so as not to dull the blade of your trimming scissors. See the chapter "Techniques to Trim Fast" for more details.

Trim Bin (G/Tr)

Trim bins or trays allow you to trim on your lap and greatly increase your work-space. There are professional models that have various compartments or an edge you can set onto the side of a table. Some models also have a screen to collect keef with, but normal plastic bins, paint roller trays, and cardboard boxes work too.

Food and Snacks (G/Tr)

Most trim scenes will supply at least one meal per day, but it is good to bring snacks, water, and drinks for yourself too.

Mask (Tr)

When working with weed that has a lot of mold or powdery mildew, or weed that has been treated with pesticides, some trimmers like wearing a mask to protect their lungs. Be aware that it is possible to develop an allergic reaction to weed itself, such as a skin reaction when working with the live plant or a respiratory reaction when trimming in an enclosed space.

THE LARF **HAS ENTERED**

MY BRAIN

Headlamp (Tr)

Good lighting helps prevent eye strain and allows you to see what needs to be trimmed better. Some trim scenes do not have the best lighting or have no artificial lighting at all, so it can be beneficial to bring a headlamp.

Clothing (Tr)

Wear clothing that is comfortable. For a shirt wear something buttonless like a t-shirt or long-sleeved shirt. Wear shoes or your feet and socks may become covered in trim and resin. The smell of weed is extremely hard to wash out, so wear clothes that you don't mind dedicating to trimming. If you're self-conscious about smelling like weed in public, consider bringing a change of clothes and something to bag up your trim clothes with. The smell of weed is best washed out with a pungent name-brand laundry detergent and a cup of white vinegar diluted in a quart of water. You can also wear an apron to try and prevent getting the oils of weed onto your clothing, but even that won't fully protect you.

BASICS FOR TRIM BOSSES AND GROWERS

Perhaps you are the trim boss and the grower, or perhaps you have been hired by the grower as a trim boss. Either way, you will be in charge of a crew of workers from a diverse background. Naturally you also have the option of trimming your weed by yourself, but this is often a timely and impractical task for moving product to market, so it is better to hire the helping scissors of trimmers.

As a trim boss it is your job to make sure the trimming goes smoothly and provide anything that the trimmers need. The only essential role of a trim boss is to make sure that the final trimmed product looks good, though beyond that trim bosses may give instruction, teach, sweep, buck down branches of weed, big leaf, cut down fresh weed for wet trimming, cook meals, trim, remove bins of stems and leaves, reload a table with more weed, process nugs through a machine trimmer, and control the music. As a trim boss there is a certain amount of etiquette to follow when hiring trimmers to work for you and when directing them around, so read up.

How Many Trimmers Should You Hire?

How many trimmers can you accommodate? How many can you instruct and direct? How many can you feed? How many can you provide lodging to? How many people do you know that you trust to trim your weed? More importantly, how much weed do you have to trim and how fast do you want it trimmed? Cannabinoids and resin glands degrade in light, hot temperatures, damp conditions, with rough handling, and over time. The sooner you get your weed trimmed, the less chance these factors have of destroying the weed's quality.

You do need to have enough work for it to be worthwhile to a trimmer. How much weed a trimmer can process per hour depends on the size and leafiness of your weed, whether or not you're using a trim machine, as well as how much work you do to help the trimmers. Without your assistance, an average trimmer can trim a dried pound of medium-sized outdoor grown weed in 8-10 hours, and twice that amount for nice medium-sized indoor grown weed. At the very least, you should give trimmers a pound of work, or 6-10 hours each. Most trimmers prefer more work than this, granted that you want to allow your workers to take periodic days off and not be trimming every day of the year.

Your state may require trimmers to be licensed to process weed, so read up on the laws. You can hire your workers as part-time employees, full-time employees, or as independent contractors. The designation changes how you handle taxes and payment in your state.

Communication

If you hire help, be sure you are forward and direct. Don't be a bucket of larf or a passive aggressive nug. Clearly communicate your needs and expectations as well as anything about food, supplies, payment, hours per day trimmers are expected to work, and how many days of work you have for them. Do this before the trim day so the trimmer can make an informed decision about whether or not they want to work for you, and so that they know exactly what they need to bring.

At the beginning of the trim session, show your trimmers a few examples of how you want your weed trimmed. Each day that a person works for you, or when you switch over to a new strain of weed, check that person's trimmed nugs and B-buds within the first hour. Even if you know that a person is a good trimmer, trimmers can have their off days, or have been trimming under a different trim boss with different expectations. It is bad etiquette to tell a trimmer halfway through the day that they need to redo their whole bag of finished nugs, and especially bad when they're fired or quietly let go of without any indication as to why. Communicate your expectations and be an active teacher! Whether or not you invite a trimmer back for future trim sessions is of course up to you.

Don't Flirt or Sleep with Your Trimmers

Seriously, this almost always ends dramatically. At least wait until the trim session is over! The same goes for anyone you are growing for. A trimmer's refusal to give you sexual favors or love does not make it legal or appropriate for you to fire them or cut their wages.

Food

Let trimmers know ahead of time whether or not you are providing food, otherwise tell them to bring their own. If you are providing food ask trimmers if they have any dietary restrictions. Watch out for feeding everyone heavy greasy food or beans; you don't want your trim room full of smelly farts or upset stomachs.

Dry to the Proper Moisture Content

Each strain of weed has an ideal moisture content to trim at, but at the very least the stems should snap. Typically dense buds are easier to trim when very dry, whereas lighter or larfy buds need to be slightly moist so as not to break apart while being handled. You can open a bin of weed in a warm and dry environment to help it dry more, or you can leave a plastic bag with a damp paper towel in the bin with the lid closed to increase the moisture content. If a bin is going to take a long time to trim, keep the lid on to maintain its moisture content. Weed dried too much or kept in temperatures over 80 degrees Fahrenheit causes some of the chemical components to dissipate, so be careful and don't allow trimmers to work in direct sunlight. Please see other materials for the proper curing and drying of weed.

Table Setup and Supplies

See the "Materials" chapter for a list of supplies. You'll need a sufficient amount for all the trimmers you are hiring. Many trimmers bring some of their own supplies, such as scissors and trim bins, but you cannot be sure. The more trimmers that are at a table, the less efficient of systems they'll be able to create, so try to give your workers some space. When this isn't possible, trimmers tend to figure it out on their own. A 6-foot to 8-foot long table can comfortably seat 4 people, although sometimes you can squeeze people onto the ends, especially if some trim bins are being used. Place paper towels, oil, alcohol, bags, bins, and scissors in easy to reach locations.

Avoid Disasters

Place cups of alcohol and oil jars into a bowl, so that if they spill, they spill into the bowl and not all over the weed. Keep bags of finished weed out of walking pathways. Fire creepy people who make you or other trimmers uncomfortable.

Trim, B-Buds, Big Leaf, and Stems

Decide what to do with your trim, B-buds, big leaf, and stems. With the limited medicinal qualities of stems and big leaf, growers usually compost or throw them out, but their weight may need to be accounted for. Some growers save B-buds to be trimmed later while others combine B-buds and trim together for processing into oil. Depending on your markets or personal needs, you may be able to combine all varieties of trim and B-buds together, but it is generally recommended to keep different strains separate.

Wet Trimming Take Down

If wet trimming, cut down enough weed from live plants to keep your trimmers occupied for up to an hour and a half at a time. Wet weed that is not trimmed fast enough will become flaccid and difficult to work with. As trimmers come close to finishing a batch, restock the bins for another round. You can also have the trimmers perform this process.

A-Buds and B-Buds

Determine what is considered an A-bud and what is considered a B-bud for the strain of weed you are having trimmed. Usually B-buds are up to dime sized or airy. This sizing changes for wet trimming, so determine what is and what is not worth the efforts of your work crew. Let your trimmers know and show them examples. Do not force trimmers to trim B-buds! Either have B-buds trimmed separately for an hourly wage or a higher per pound payment, or just have your B-buds converted into oil or hash. Nobody likes trimming B-buds, they are not worth the time or effort to process for trimmers being paid for weight.

Music

Music helps keep the vibes up and trimmers working faster. Feel free to play your own music, but let the trim crew take over the music selection if asked.

Lodgings

If you have multiple days of work, you can offer trimmers to stay the night, either in your personally provided lodgings, or if you have land, by telling trimmers to bring camping supplies.

Payment

There are a number of different ways you can pay trimmers, just be sure that you are upfront about how you are paying them, how much you are paying them, and when they can expect to receive said pay. Even if you are recording payment details yourself, have trimmers do so as well just in case you lose your sheet, it happens!

Traditionally trimmers are paid between 8 and 20 percent of what you, the grower, sell your trimmed weed for. For instance, if you sell your weed for $2000 per pound, you would pay the trimmer $160 to $250 per pound. These numbers are fluctuating and dependent on your location, but as of 2016 payment to trimmers in the USA typically ranges between $150 and $250 per pound of trimmed dry weed, or $15 to $25 per hour worked. It's really up to you how much you pay, but higher wages often translate into higher quality or speedier work depending on what you're looking for. Many of the best trimmers won't work for low wages, or will leave trim scenes where they aren't earning enough on smaller varieties of weed, so choose your pricing carefully. You might even alter the payment amount depending on the difficulty of the strain being worked on. Below are five payment styles you can choose from:

● Hourly

A set, hourly pay is generally used for wet trimming. You can have trimmers record their own hours or you can do so yourself. Set a lunchtime and allow periodic short breaks. Hourly pay tends to create more cooperation between trimmers; for instance, trimmers can buck down as a team rather than individually and everyone can share the same bags.

● Weight

Payment per pound of weed trimmed is generally used for dry trimming. Weigh each trimmer's bag of trimmed weed at the end of the day or at the end of a strain, subtract out the bag's original weight, and record. Typically this number is recorded in grams (technically grams is a mass and not a weight, but on Earth most scales convert between pounds, kilograms, ounces, and grams just fine). See the chart at the end of this guide for metric and English unit conversions. Alternatively, some growers dry wet trimmed weed and then pay by the pound.

● Hourly Weight

Some trim scenes require trimmers to trim a specified minimum amount of weed per hour or else face consequences such as being fired. The payment may be hourly or by weight at these jobs.

● Sliding Scale (Weight/Hour)

You can create a sliding scale hourly pay based on your ideal time it takes to trim a pound of weed. This system accommodates different trimming abilities and accounts for work already done on weed such as bucking down or big leafing. For instance, you might want to pay $165 for a pound of weed (roughly 453 grams) trimmed every 8 hours. Divide the weight by the number of hours:

453grams/8hours = 56.62grams/hour
Then divide the monetary amount by the number of hours:
$165/8hours=$20.63/hour
Thus, trimming 56.62 grams/hour would earn trimmers $20.63/hour.

Based on these numbers we can use cross multiplication to figure out an individual trimmer's hourly pay. Let's figure out the pay for someone who trims 500 grams in 10 hours. Take the weight and divide it by the hours:

500grams / 10hours = 50 grams/hour
Then cross multiply this number with the original pay scale:

56.62grams/$20.63 = 50grams/X
56.62X=1031.5
X = 1031.5/56.62 = $18.21/hour

Thus, trimming 50 grams/hour would earn trimmers $18.21/hour.

Of course, the sliding scale you create must reflect the average amount of time a strain of weed takes to trim. You may have to spend a few hours figuring out the average speed of trimmers and then setup the sliding scale if you haven't worked with a strain previously. This scale may also change if you have already bucked down the weed for trimmers or done similar processing work beforehand. The sliding scale system has its benefits but also is a lot of numbers to keep track of, especially if you're working with multiple strains.

● Trade

Some trimmers want to be paid partially or fully in weed. Figure out how much you are selling your pounds for and deduct it from the trimmer's total pay. You can also pay your trimmers fully in weed, just be sure they know that they won't receive money for their work.

FASTER

TIGHTER

FASTER

TIGHTER

FASTER

TIGHTER

FASTER

BASICS OF TRIMMING
UNDER A GROWER
OR TRIM BOSS

Finding and Choosing Work

Prior to working in the trimming industry, read up about the city, county, state, and federal laws. You may be required to hold a special permit or license to trim. Knowing the laws will also help you distinguish between legal medical or recreational operations and illegal grows that you could get in trouble working for. You may be hired onto a crew as an employee or work as an independent contractor.

People find trimming jobs in a variety of ways. Typically they are found by word of mouth from friends, but you can locate job offers in dispensaries and on websites like Craigslist as well, especially around late September. People have also been known to stand on the roadside with signs asking for work, but that's sketchy.

When you connect with potential work, ask questions about payment, food, the quality of weed, the amount of work, and so on.

If you don't know the client well or cannot ask them questions before a trim session, be wary. There are a lot of weird and unprofessional growers who may not pay you. If possible ask your friends about the person or upon arriving at the job site ask the other trimmers. If you don't feel comfortable, things seem dangerous, or the weed's quality is not worth your time, leave and find other work. Sometimes though you'll start off with bad weed and move onto better trimming later. Sometimes people are just weird or unprofessional, but overall safe and will pay you. Use your best trimmer judgment.

Arrival

Job sites can be out in very obscure locations, but you may be able to get rides from the grower or other trimmers if you don't have a car. Growers prefer fewer cars parked at the grow or trim site, so carpool when possible. Upon arrival the trim room will generally be setup already. If it isn't, help unfold chairs and tables, load jars with oil and alcohol, and get out scissors, paper towels, paper bags, and turkey bags. If the trim room is already set up, prepare any items you personally brought such as a portable music player or pillow and find a seat.

Trim Boss Instructions

The trim boss will bring out weed in bins to be processed and instruct you how they want it trimmed or show you an example. Once you begin trimming the trim boss will periodically check your finished product and ask for corrections or say "that looks dank."

Etiquette

Many unique personalities come gather around the trim table, and so it's important to keep the peace by following certain guidelines:

- Smoking Weed

Certain state laws may restrict the smoking of weed at your trim job, but generally trim bosses are fine with you lighting up so long as you remain semi-functional. People who smoke may become silent and untalkative, or say strange and confusing things. Other people trim better stoned depending on the variety of weed and how much they smoke.

- Conversation

All sorts of interesting conversations come up while working, especially when people are stoned or slowly losing their minds staring at small shrubs a foot from their faces for too many hours straight. Try not to get into arguments, and for that matter avoid voicing strong opinions. Don't flirt with people. Don't yell. Don't force people into conversations who are remaining silent. Just do your best to make people feel comfortable. It's already hard enough work as it is without people being annoying! Also keep conversations and people's identities confidential. Weed is a sensitive topic and people may bring up personal information. To respect the grower as well, you never tell anyone the location of where you are working or who you are working for. Have a backup story ready.

- Music

Often trim bosses will have a music player of some kind. Sometimes they will exclusively control the music, but generally you can ask to put on your own tunes. Upbeat music is best to play. Avoid comedy routines, what's funny to you may be offensive or annoying to someone else. Feel free to bring your own portable music player and cut out the surrounding conversations or music with headphones. Just don't have the volume so high that other people have to listen to your music and the main music player at the same time.

- Reload the Table

When your pile of weed becomes depleted and you've cleaned off the remains, go grab more from the bin. If the bin is empty, inform the trim boss that you need more.

● Cherry Picking (DON'T DO IT!)

Not all weed is grown to the same size, and some trimmers will "cherry pick" a bin for the branches with the biggest buds. Don't do this! If people catch you cherry picking you will be labeled as a terrible person. Just grab a handful or armload of the branches at the top of the bin and return to your workstation. Cherry picking may also refer to throwing especially large buds into the B-bud bag.

● Your Pile

While working for weight, you'll generally want to keep your bucked down buds for yourself. If you're being paid an hourly wage, a more communal trim can happen with everyone bucking down a pile of branches together and then trimming that pile of bucked down buds. Periodically people will communally buck down while working for weight, but this often seems to slow people down.

● Help New Trimmers

If you are sitting with someone who is new to trimming try to give them some pointers, or tell them to watch how you trim for a few minutes.

● Keep Your Scissors To Yourself

Don't grab other trimmer's scissors unless you've received permission to. If you're using scissors supplied by the trim boss, stick with those scissors and think about how you're immediately going to purchase your own pair once you're finished working that day.

● Wash Your Hands

You should not only wash your hands after using the bathroom or eating, but also before rubbing your eyes or strumming a guitar! Otherwise your eyes will burn and you'll have to replace those sticky strings.

● Nighttime

If you are staying over or working late, use green lights when interacting with or passing by live weed plants at night.

● Be Careful with Alcohol and Oil!

Alcohol and oil, while great for cleaning scissors, will destroy weed if spilled. Take measures to prevent containers of alcohol and oil from spilling, either by having them on a separate table or having their containers in a bowl or another container. If you do happen to knock over a jar of oil or alcohol and destroy someone's bucked down or trimmed weed, replace what you destroyed and apologize to the trim boss.

● Taking Days Off

If you leave a trim scene for several days or plan to work intermittently throughout the month, your position may be given away. Communicate with the grower or trim boss for specifics.

Food

The owner of a grow will typically supply you with at least one meal a day, and two or three if you're living on-site. This is not always amazing food so prepare your own if you have any food restrictions. Either way, bring snacks and water or some sort of drink to keep you going throughout the day. Generally food that you can eat quickly is best.

Cleanup

Once you're finished for the day, give your scissors a good wipe down, fold up the chairs, sweep the floor, and clean your hands.

Records

This is how you are paid! At the end of the day get the number of hours you worked or weight you trimmed recorded with the trim boss. Sometimes the trim boss does this daily and other times they weigh your bags from several days of work. Either way, keep your own daily record. Growers and trim bosses have been known to misplace or lose the records they keep so don't rely on them.

Payment

You may be paid hourly, per pound trimmed, on a sliding scale, or in trade. See "Payment Types" under "Basics for Trim Bosses and Growers" for specifics. Note that even if a job is low-paying you will never know how profitable it is until seeing the size of the nugs and how much processing must be done to the weed. Sometimes the pay is less per pound if the weed is already bucked down, but that allows you to work faster. Also keep in mind that growers may have to sell the weed first before they can pay you, so be patient. Confirm the time frame for receiving your payment prior to beginning work. If the average payment in your state becomes particularly low, it may be worthwhile to form a trimmer's union to guarantee wages and benefits for yourself and other trimmers.

Reintegration Into Society

Trim work immerses you into a weird world that does strange things to your mind. The conversations that you have, intensely staring at nugs for hours on end, sitting in uncomfortable chairs, frustrations with the quality of weed, and other factors all influence your mental health and ability to relate to the normal world. Many people call it "larf brain" or "trim fever." Just take it easy at first: shower, eat a proper meal, close your eyes and take a nap, reintroduce your eyes to natural lighting, and avoid telling any trimmer jokes or conspiracy theories to your friends and family. Be extremely careful driving. If you start feeling depressed at any point, consider reading my book, "The Happiest Choice: Essential Tools For Everyone's Brain Feelings" or "YOU ARE A GREAT AND POWERFUL WIZARD."

TRIM TIGHTNESS

Loose: a few larger leaves remain.

Untrimmed

Loose-Tight: a few extra leaves remain for aesthetic flair.

Tight: only sugar leaf and hairs remain and all dark green has been removed.

Too tight: most of the outer sugar leaf has been shaved off.

PROBLEMS TO LOOK FOR

Mold appears as a dull yellow, fuzzy white, grey, or brown patch and is often found on the inside of a nug.

Mites are various colors when alive and then shrivel into little balls. They can leave yellow splotching and and webbing.

Leaf yellowing or leaf burn appears as a yellowing or browning of the leaf but can generally be trimmed out.

Powdery mildew coats leaves with splotches of white and is easily confused with a nug that is dense with trichomes.

1   The Stoner Bro: He's macho and stoned. Sometimes surfs.

2   The Functional Stoner: Trims just as well or better after smoking.

3   The Student: Funds their education with money from trimming.

4   The Dysfunctional Stoner: Smokes weed and cannot speak sensibly or trim with any speed.

5   The Spiritualist: Meditates, drinks smoothies, and stretches all over the place.

TRIMMER

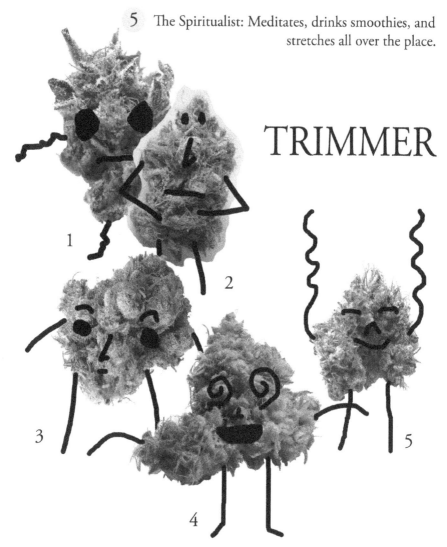

6   The Traveler: Sometimes foreign, drops in on the trim scene to fund their world travels.

7   The Conspiracy Theorist: Divulges how everything around you is trying to manipulate and control your mind.

8   The Grow-Ho: Sleeps with the grower or trim boss and receives special treatment as a result.

9   The Non-Smoker: Trims up a storm but doesn't ever smoke weed.

10   Festival Goer: Always about to go to another festival.

STEREOTYPES

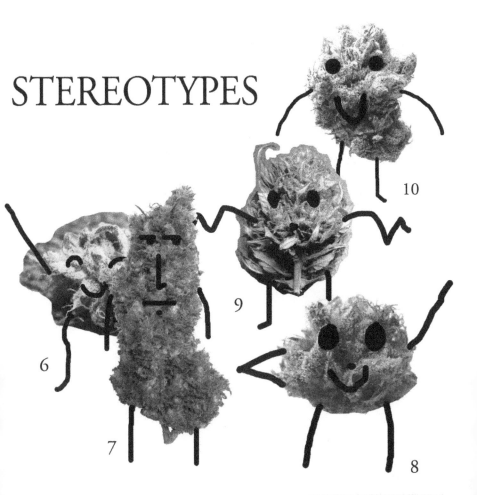

HOW TO TRIM

Now that you're familiar with setting up a trim station and what to expect at trim scenes, let's talk about how to trim. You or your trim boss will grab a pile of weed from a bin and place it within arm's reach for you to process. This might be in the form of wet branches, dried branches, bucked down buds, or machine trimmed buds that need to be trimmed more. There should be enough weed for you to stay busy for at least half an hour, but not too much that it makes your space cluttered. Depending on the number of people and size of nugs, anywhere from 5-15 branches should be sufficient. You're ready to start trimming. Note that this section covers the basics of trimming while the next covers advanced trimming techniques.

Step 0) Powdery Mildew, Mites, Mold, and Miscellaneous Problems

Throughout the whole process of trimming be on the lookout for powdery mildew, mites, mold, and various other problems such as leaf burn and smashed nugs. For photos see the chapter "Problems To Look For." Check in with the trim boss if you see something suspicious but you're not sure what it is. Separate any nugs you find with these problems, they are generally put with the bare stems to be burned, composted, or thrown away. Some of these problems will cause weed to fail lab tests and cannot be sold. In order to help prevent the spread of these contaminants after trimming, shower before handling live weed plants.

- Mold or bud rot appears as a discoloration on a nug. Often brown, a dull yellow around the nug's center, and/or a fuzzy white, moldy spots may be soft and can be pressed in. Especially inspect the insides of larger nugs.
- Powdery mildew appears as a white powder on leaves, but can easily be confused with sprays that have been applied and dried onto a nug, or a nug with lots of trichomes. Some growers may have you wash off powdery mildew by dunking the weed into hydrogen peroxide and drying it.
- Mites appear as many tiny dots on leaves. Sometimes they are still alive and moving around, other times they are dead.
- Leaf burn happens for a variety of reasons and must be cut out. It appears as a yellowing or browning of the leaf.
- Larf refers to a nug that is airy or not dense.

Step 1) Big Leaf
Big leafing is the process of removing the largest fan leaves from a branch of weed. This can be done on the living plant before harvest, once the plant is cut down wet, or once the weed has dried. Preferably big leafing is done earlier on as it helps speed the drying process.

Cut the fan leaves with scissors or pruners, or pluck them off with your hands. Often this step can be skipped, but is something trim bosses instruct trimmers to do. Take care not to mix big leaf and stems in with the sugar leaf trim because it will lower the quality of concentrates and oils when the trim is processed.

Step 2) Buck Down

Bucking down is the act of removing nugs from a branch of weed, either wet or dry, to have them ready to trim by hand or machine. Generally this is done with scissors, but sometimes you can pluck them off with your fingers if the stems are dry enough. Do the pluck and chuck!

If the size of the plants or branches are difficult to work with, cut them down to something more manageable. Work up from the base of the branch, twirling the branch between your fingers as the pattern of the nug stems rotate side to side. Toss out any moldy or mildewy nugs you find. As you buck down, separate A-buds from B-buds. Do not throw a branch full of B-buds into the B-bud bag; they must be separated. Stems and big leaf do NOT go into the B-bud bag. Every trim boss will have a different idea of what constitutes a B-bud but generally B-buds trim down to smaller than a dime

and/or are too larfy. Keep in mind while wet trimming that the nugs will shrink and may expose more stem than is desirable. Different trim bosses will also want different sizes of A-buds. Even if a large bud would look nice and tight, a buyer may desire smaller buds. That said, the image below on the left is generally considered a B-bud and the image on the right an A-bud.

You can also communally buck down, but people generally only do this when being paid hourly. Sometimes a kindly trim boss will take care of bucking down or partially bucking down for you.

How much do you break an individual nug down? A general rule of thumb is to break down a bud until you can no longer see through any of the bud's central body. This may not be apparent until trimming off some leaves. Often a nug is also broken down if the main stem can be seen through the foliage. If the main stem only shows

through on one side, or breaking the bud down would make it a B-bud, an exception can be made depending on the directions of the trim boss. Of course, the more you break a nug down, the more work you have. Even if a large nug would look nice and tight, some growers will have you break down a nug more because of what a specific buyer wants. Try to keep nugs as large as your trim boss will allow. In the picture to the left, the bottom three or four nugs need to be bucked down.

If trimming from the stem, cut branches into 6 to 12 inch lengths or buck nugs down with a little extra stem on the end to hold onto. If you leave the buds on the branch, make sure you can access all the leaves needing to be trimmed. After the trimming process buck the nugs down straight into your finished container or to the side for a second workaround.

Step 3) Snip Off The Base Stem
You want a short base stem, 1-2 millimeters in length, so it doesn't poke through plastic bags. Don't cut the stem so short that it makes the nug fall apart. You can postpone this step until after trimming the bud's leaves to help prevent breakage for more sensitive strains. The stem in the first image is too long and the stem in the image to the right is perfect.

For machine trimming, you want a longer stem, at least a quarter-inch in length, otherwise the machine trimmer will break the nug apart. After being run through the trim machine you can then snip the stem to an appropriate length.

Step 4) Snip Off The Crow's Feet

The crow's feet are located on the underside of the nug. They are the first set of leaves branching off from the base stem. Most but not all nugs have these.

Step 5) Snip Off The Protruding Stems

Several leaves will have thick stems attached to the central nug stem. With your scissors reach in through the foliage and cut them out. This process can be combined with the next step.

Step 6) Trim Leaves by Hand or Machine

If machine trimming, follow your trim machine's instructions to process the prepared weed. Generally only one or two individuals will handle this and then touch-up whatever comes out.

If hand trimming, trim to the desired tightness as described previously in "Types of Trimming" and "Trim Tightness." Sometimes the goal of trimming will be to remove or hide any big or dark green leaves that contain little to no trichomes, otherwise the goal is to shape the bud into a smooth and continuous form. Hold the bud in one hand and snip or cleave the leaves off while you rotate it, cutting up and down or spiraling upward starting from the base. You want to quickly move your scissors across the nug as you snip to knock the trimmed leaves away from the nug. This will create a fast back and forth motion. Avoid moving your scissors up and down away from the nug. Good trimmers snip their scissors 2-5 times per second. Avoid trimming directly over your bucked down nugs!

38

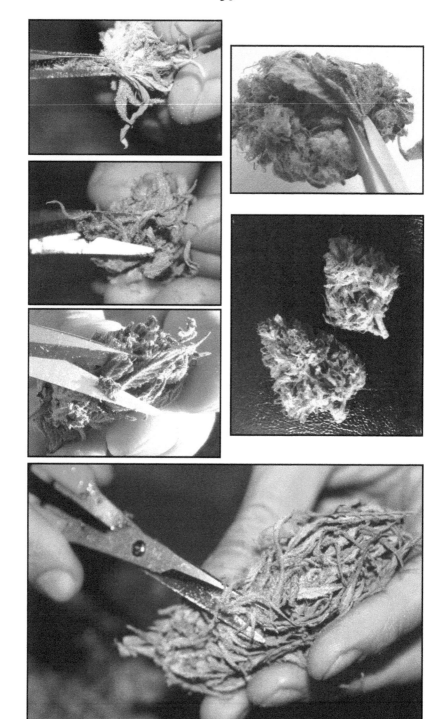

If trimming from the stem, follow the same procedure but hold onto the bud's base stem or the woody part of a branch of nugs while trimming. If you have trouble keeping the bud still, hold it against the table, brace it with your index finger, or brace your forearm against the table. After trimming the bud, snip off the extra stem or buck off the finished nugs straight into your trimmed container of weed.

As your scissors get gunked up and sticky, clean them with a plant-based oil and/or isopropyl alcohol. Cut out or separate any nugs you find with powdery mildew or mold. Place anything that forms a B-bud into the B-bud bag. If the weed is dry enough you can alternate between trimming with your fingers and scissors. Certain strains can be finger trimmed by brushing the leaves off with your index finger. Alternatively you can brush with your scissors open or closed. Other strains may require some plucking.

Step 7) Clean Nug
Some varieties of weed are really sticky and the trimmed leaves stay on the bud instead of falling down. Pick this off with your scissors or hands or blow it off with your mouth.

Step 8) Bag Finished Nug

Gently place the finished nugs in a bag or other container. This bag should be located close to you as well as in a place that trim won't fall into and safe from foot traffic and spilled liquids. A turkey bag inside of a paper grocery bag or bucket tucked underneath the table is generally safe from these dangers. Alternatively you can use a sealable bin as described previously in the materials chapter. Many trimmers like to first place finished nugs into a small container which is then emptied into their main bag. At the end of the day take five minutes to pick out any stems or leaves that have fallen into your bag, cleanup any glaring mistakes on your trimmed nugs, and remove big leaf from the sugar leaf trim.

Step 9) Clean Work Area and Hands

You'll want to periodically clean your work area and hands. When your scissors start to stick together from the resin, let them soak in a cup of oil and/or alcohol for several minutes before taking them out and wiping the blades down with a paper towel or cloth. Alternatively you can burn the resin off with a lighter and wait for the metal to cool, but this may compromise the blades' sharpness over time. Never clean your scissors with water or leave them soaking in alcohol overnight! When the scissor bolt becomes sticky, flip your scissors upside down after removing them from the container of oil or alcohol and snip several times until the bolt is loosened.

Most growers want to keep the small trim you've cut off from buds, so bag this up in the trim bag. Toss big leaves and stems into another bag or bin to be composted or burned (see the photo above). If necessary remove big or yellow leaves and stems from the trim. Toss B-buds into a B-bud bag. Some trim bosses keep different varieties of weed trim separate and others mix it all together.

When you're done for the day you can wash the table with isopropyl alcohol and sweep up the ground. Clean your hands by rubbing them with oil and then washing with soap and warm water. Note that you and your clothes are going to smell like weed after trimming. You might not smell it yourself after being around weed for so long, but you definitely smell of weed. If this makes you self-conscious, wash your hands twice, change your clothes, and shower as soon as possible.

Step 10) Dry or Cure Trimmed Weed

If wet trimmed, the weed now needs to be dried. If dry trimmed, the weed now needs to be cured. Please see other resources for the proper drying and curing of weed. Just know that cannabinoids and resin glands degrade in light, hot temperatures, damp conditions, with rough handling, and over time, so be careful.

ALL OF THE TREES ARE GIANT BUDS AND NEED TRIMMING

TECHNIQUES TO TRIM FAST

Legend has it that there is one who can merely whisper to nugs and the leaves fall off unveiling a perfectly trimmed A-bud. For the rest of us, trimming weed is fairly simple, but it is the steps that you take with each branch, stem, nug, and leaf that determines how fast you can work. Remember that every split second saved adds up over the course of hours. Many techniques will come to you through observation and asking questions, but many others require practice and muscle memory. It is only with time that you will discover the best tactics for various strains of wet or dry weed, so get to trimming!

Maintain Endurance

Even trimming for a single 8 to 12 hour day can injure or irritate your hands, back, eyes, and mind. This will only be exacerbated if you're working for weeks non-stop, so take some basic steps to maintain your endurance and prevent larf brain or trim fever:

- Remember to eat or snack throughout the day so that your blood sugar doesn't crash. Also remember that you're not moving or burning many calories, so you don't need that much food. It's easy to take too many breaks and waste time.
- If your hands start to hurt wear a wrist brace at night. Alternatively you can sleep with your hands lying flat instead of curled up. Icing your wrists also helps.
- Take breaks where you stretch your hands and your back. Also take this time to stare off into the distance and get some fresh air.
- Exchange a massage with another trimmer or take a visit to the local massage therapist.
- Build your core so you don't throw out your back from sitting for so long.
- Purchase a pillow or two to make an uncomfortable chair into something more bearable.
- It's easy to become distracted and unmotivated while working. Say a mantra such as "faster, faster!" to perk back up. You can also repeat positive things to yourself.
- Use good scissors. If you're using spring-loaded scissors, you may want to cut the spring shorter to make it easier to snip with and release unneeded pressure on your hand.
- Smoke weed only if you know you can work better high. Many people work slower while high, especially if they're trying to keep up a conversation.
- Listen to upbeat music.
- Sit next to someone who snips their scissors faster than you as a constant reminder that you could be moving faster.
- Stand up while trimming to get some blood moving and relax your back and behind.

Keep Focus

People have varying abilities at keeping focused while multitasking, but you will trim fastest and learn the best when you concentrate your focus onto the bud. Go into full focus mode periodically in order to re-boost your efficiency and automate it while you're distracted:

- Limit talking or learn how to work and talk simultaneously.
- Limit being distracted by food or taking too long of breaks.
- Wear headphones.
- Don't play movies.
- Face a wall so you don't constantly look at the cute trimmers.

Find The Right Scene

As you trim more you'll receive extra work and eventually have to choose between different people to work for.

- Work for someone who grows good weed with big buds and allows you to separate out B-buds.
- Find a trim boss who will buck down buds for you.
- Find a workplace that treats you well, is comfortable, has good food, plays good music, and has enjoyable people.
- Find a workplace that has a lot of weed and few trimmers.

Multitask While Bucking Down

You can save a lot of time by combining several steps in the process of bucking down.

- Buck down without big leafing. Sometimes it's harder to see where to cut the nugs, but often there's no need to big leaf.
- While bucking down separate B-buds from A-buds. After you've worked with a strain for a short period of time, you'll be able to see that some buds that initially appear to be whole A-buds actually have some B-buds at the base.
- Buck down a large pile of nugs to work on before starting to trim leaves and stems off.

- Snip the bud stems to the desired length in the bucking down process to avoid having to repeat cutting the stem while trimming.
- While bucking down, cut through the nug stem and main branch instead of finding each branching point and keeping the branch intact. This is most easily done by holding onto the top kola

and working up from the base of the branch. While faster, using this method can create a mess that you'll later have to cleanup so be careful.

Position Materials Efficiently

A system that flows and allows you to easily access and move buds and materials will help speed up your trimming process.

- If you're holding a bud with your left hand, place your finished bin on your left.
- If you hold your scissors with your right hand, place your alcohol and oil to your right.
- Instead of placing each trimmed nug into your finished bag, place them into a short plastic container (2-5 inches in height) on your table or trim bin and then dump the filled container into your finished bag. If possible position the container at or above the level of your hands in order to prevent leaves and stems from falling in.
- Combine your isopropyl alcohol and oil into one jar. You're now applying both whenever you soak your scissors.
- Bring a trim bin, either professional or makeshift. Just because you're using a trim bin doesn't mean you can't use the table though, spread out your materials!

Scissors

- Have two or three pairs of scissors, marked to separate them from other scissors, that you take care of and use exclusively for trimming. Replace pairs that begin getting dull, or devote a dull pair to bucking down and cutting through branches.

- Switch between pairs of scissors, letting the gunked up pair soak in isopropyl alcohol and/or oil. If your scissors aren't too gunked up they can simply be dunked in alcohol and toweled off before being used again.

- If you don't have access to alcohol, it may be better to scrape resin off of scissors with your fingernail or an x-acto blade, especially for varieties of weed that gunk up scissors fast.

- Wear a sock with the bottom cut out around your forearm to wipe your scissors clean of oil, alcohol, and weed. This makes it so that you don't have to reach for a paper towel each time you clean your scissors.

- Purchase a good pair of scissors. A favorite in the trim scene is the curved Chikamasa scissors available at many weed dispensaries and grow shops. The curve hugs the nug like a good friend. Two other popular pairs are the angled Chikamasa and angled ARS scissors. There are also spring-loaded curved and angled scissors if you prefer those; they are useful for sticky nugs. All of these specialty scissors are expensive but worth it.

- While trimming bud leaves you should be snipping at the very least twice per second, but some people snip 5 or more times per second depending on the type of weed being trimmed. The difference in speed takes the form of calculated, large swath cuts or many small cuts for details. A middle ground creates the nicest and fastest trimmed nugs.

- Keep your scissors close to the nug, moving your scissors side-to-side across the nug rather than up-and-down away and toward it.
- While using your fingers to pluck or trim, you will still need your scissors periodically. Rather than putting your scissors down, loop your thumb through the top portion to allow good mobility with both your fingers and scissors.

Do the Appropriate Amount of Work

Out of all other suggestions in this guide, these will save you the most time. Each trim scene expects a different work speed and trim tightness. If you've been working multiple trim gigs it's easy to work too slow, work too fast, trim too tight, or trim too loose. In general though:

- Start looser and then get tighter if the trim boss tells you to.
- Watch how other trimmers work.
- Ask to see examples of other trimmer's finished nugs.
- Once you get into the swing of things, do not double check your work until the very end of the day. When you've made a full rotation around a bud, put it in your finished pile and move on. At the end of the day, quickly go through your bag to fix any glaring mistakes and remove big leaves or stems that have fallen in.
- Some people set a limit to the number of snips they use per nug, but this can quickly lead to bad trimming. It might work when you perfect your technique for a specific strain though and is useful as a reminder not to spend too much time on one nug.

- It's unfortunate to say, but sometimes a trim boss will tell you to trim tighter when that either isn't possible or isn't what anyone, even a person in high standing at the trim table, is doing. Of course, some trimmers get special treatment or don't ever have their bags of trimmed nugs checked, so can get away with sloppier trim jobs. Ignoring the trim boss may jeopardize your job, so use your own discretion, but sometimes they have to be ignored.

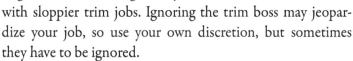

- A similar statement can be made about A-buds and B-buds. A trim boss may ask for extremely small buds to be trimmed that are simply not worth your time or effort. Sometimes this is an unavoidable pain that must be endured until a strain that didn't grow so well is finished being trimmed. That said, separate out what you can as B-buds.
- These past two points aside, working above and beyond what is expected will get you invited back and invited to other trim scenes. Trimming fast and tight will earn you respect at trim scenes. Being a likable person and having a flexible schedule helps too.
- Certain strains of weed immediately gunk up your scissors and fingers, and so it becomes inefficient to constantly clean them. Experiment with not cleaning your hands or scissors of resin.
- Keep your fingers very lightly oiled.
- If you are dealing with a lot of larf, B-buds, and mold in already bucked down weed, sort through it first instead of individually plucking out good buds to trim.

Trimming

- Use the appropriate techniques for the weed being trimmed whether that be scissor trimming, finger trimming, bucking off nugs with your hands or snipping them off with your scissors, using oil or using alcohol, etc.
- Bucking down may be easier with a branch held against the table rather than in the air.
- On buds that break apart easily, cut the stem last so as not to accidentally destroy the whole bud. You can also hold the bud with an additional amount of pressure so that it does not fall apart.
- Rent a trim machine.
- Find a machine to trim B-buds with.
- Find a machine to trim spherical A-buds with. You can also partially trim oddly shaped buds through a machine trimmer and then have trimmers touch up the nooks and crannies.
- Try turning the bud upside down to better access the nooks and crannies.
- Pick up multiple buds at a time to work on.
- Trimming branches of weed in 6 to 8 inch sections and then bucking the partially or fully trimmed nugs off helps trim B-buds since you trim them with the A-buds. If the stems are dry enough you can buck the buds off into your finished bin by leveraging your scissors between the bud and main branch instead of snipping them off.
- Water weed to be wet trimmed the day of or day before cutting it down. After removing branches, keep them out of the sun, in a cool environment, and not stacked up too high until they can be processed.
- Cut your fingernails before starting to trim.
- If too much trim and big leaf falls into your finished bag of nugs, dump everything out and separate out the gunk.
- For some strains you can cut one of the crow's feet and the stem at the same time.

I AM
ONE WITH
THE NUG

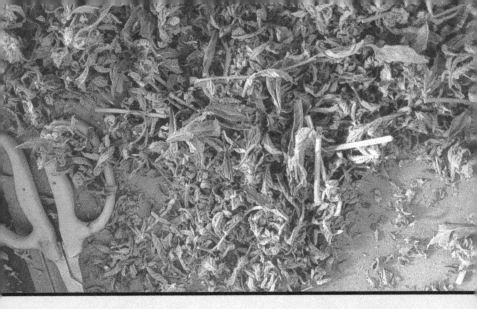

GLOSSARY

A-Bud
Buds that are good enough and large enough to trim.

Base Stem
The bottom of a nug's stem up to where it branches out.

B-Bud
Buds, typically dime sized or smaller after being trimmed. Might also be larfy. They are not worthwhile to trim and growers usually convert them into oil or hash, or have them trimmed separately.

Big Leaf
Refers to the fan leaves and bigger leaves on a weed plant. Might also be used as a verb to refer to "big leafing."

Big Leafing
The act of removing the medium to largest leaves on a branch of ganja. This is generally done before the drying process.

Branch

A stem with many buds on it. "Branch" is used in this booklet to differentiate from the stem on an individual bud. Generally you will hear people refer to branches as stems.

Bud

The flower of a cannabis plant. Bud may also refer to a unit of weed that forms a continues shape and does not expose much stem.

Bucking Down

The process of removing buds from a branch of weed.

Bud Rot

See "mold."

Cannabinoid

A set of various chemicals produced by cannabis plants, including THC and CBD.

CBD (Cannabidiol)

A type of cannabinoid in cannabis that some research shows having anti-inflammatory and anti-psychotic properties. Creates a body high.

Cannabis

The scientific name for weed. Cannabis may refer to cannabis with medicinal properties (weed/herb/marijuana/ganja), or cannabis with structural and material properties (hemp). There are three species of cannabis: C. sativa, C. indica, and C. ruderalis. These species can be crossed into hybrids.

Cherry Picking

At a trim scene, the act of individually selecting the biggest nugs for yourself. This is extremely frowned upon.

Chopping
See "take down."

Chronic
High quality weed. Also a specific strain of cannabis, and on the east coast of the USA, weed mixed with cocaine.

Cola/Kola
The top bud of a branch of weed, generally the biggest.

Crow's Feet
The leaves with large stems protruding from the base of a nug.

Dank
Especially good.

Fan Leaves
The biggest leaves on a cannabis plant. May also be referred to as the big leaf.

Frosty
When a nug is dense with white trichomes. Not to be confused with powdery mildew.

Ganja
A Sanskrit word for weed.

Hemp
A type of cannabis with structural and material properties rather than medicinal ones.

Herb

Usually refers to medicinal cannabis that has been dried and is ready to smoke or consume some other way.

Indoor Grow

Weed grown indoors. Typically indoor grown weed is nicer to trim and can be sold for a higher price than outdoor grown weed.

Keef/Kief

Keef is the white crystals or trichomes that have fallen off a nug. Some growers have trimmers collect this to make products out of.

Kola

See Cola.

Lab Test

To legally sell weed, trimmed nugs must be sent to a lab facility for an inspection of various problems as well as the levels of THC, CBD, and other chemicals.

Larf/Larfy

Weed that is airy and not dense.

Larf Brain

A type of mental fatigue that happens after trimming for many hours.

Leaf Burn

Browning and yellowing on leaves resulting from a variety of problems. Needs to be cut out while trimming.

Marijuana

Marijuana typically refers to a whole cannabis plant grown for medicinal purposes or to cannabis buds with medicinal properties. The term marijuana is considered by some to be offensive because it was originally anglicized from Mexican immigrants in order to discriminate against several groups of people and make all cannabis illegal. Marijuana is synonymous with herb and weed.

Mold

Also known as bud rot. It appears as a gray or brown discoloration on a nug that is soft and can be pressed in. Moldy spots of weed will cause lab tests to fail and must be discarded.

Nug

A unit of weed that forms a continuous shape and does not expose much stem. Typically a nug refers to a bud that has already been dried and trimmed.

Nug Crushing

Crushing a nug into trim or a B-bud that is between an A-bud and B-bud but not quite worth the trimmer's time to deal with. Might also be performed on larfy buds. Don't get caught doing this.

Outdoor Grow

Weed grown outdoors. Greenhouse grown weed may also be considered outdoor, but not always.

Powdery Mildew

A fungal disease that appears as white splotches on leaves. If too much is on the final batch of trimmed nugs it will cause a lab test to fail.

Resin

Primarily contained within the trichomes of mature weed plants. When handling buds this is the black residue that sticks to your fingers.

Shake

Keef and sugar leaf that have been trimmed off of nugs. Shake is still good to smoke or use in creating products, but can be more difficult to sell than trimmed weed.

Shaving

Shaving a nug involves cutting large swaths with scissors which removes much of the exterior sugar leaf and trichomes. Shaving too much is generally looked down upon but is a fast way of trimming.

Stems

In this booklet, stems refer to the small woody parts of a bud, but at a trim scene it may mean a branch of cannabis that has been stripped down bare and can be burned or composted.

Sugar Leaf/Sweet Leaf

Leaves of a bud with trichomes.

Take Down

Also known as chopping. The act of cutting branches off a living cannabis plant to either dry or to wet trim. These branches are normally 12-24 inches in length or small enough to fit into a plastic bin for transport.

Tar

The residue left in a pipe after weed is smoked from it.

Terpene

Chemicals in weed that provides it with aroma and flavor.

THC (Tetrahydrocannabinol)

A type of cannabinoid in cannabis that has psychoactive properties. Creates a head high.

Totes
Bins used for a variety of weed responsibilities.

Trichomes
The white crystals on a nug that contain the majority of the CBD, THC, and other chemicals found in weed. Trichomes fall off easily so trimmers may be instructed to take special precautions while handling the buds.

Trim
The outer leaves of a bud that you trim off to shape it. Can be smoked, used to make oil, or hash.

Trim Bin
Trim bins allow you to trim on your lap and greatly increase your workspace. There are professional models that have various compartments or an edge you can set onto the side of a table. Some models also have a screen to collect keef with, but normal plastic bins or cardboard boxes work too.

Trim Boss
The person in charge of directing trimmers at a trim scene. Not necessarily the grower.

Trim Fever
See "larf brain."

Trim Room
A room in which trimming takes place.

Turkey Bags
A type of strong and clear plastic bag commonly used to place trimmed buds and trim into.

Weed

Weed typically refers to a whole cannabis plant grown for medicinal purposes, to cannabis buds with medicinal properties, or to trimmed cannabis buds. It has many other names including ganja, Mary Jane, marijuana, and herb.

WEIGHT AND MASS REFERENCES FOR WEED

The following numbers are conversions between common measurements used in the weed industry. Be warned though that weight (pounds and ounces) is gravity-based and changes between planets. On the other hand, mass (grams and kilograms) stays constant wherever in the universe you are. If you need to convert between these metric and English units on a planet other than Earth please see a separate reference guide as the following numbers will be inaccurate.

1 pound (lb) = 16 ounces (oz)
1 pound (lb) = 453.592 grams (g)
1 pound (lb) = .453592 kilograms (kg)
"A quarter pound" = 4 ounces (oz) = 113.398 grams (g)
"A half pound" = 8 ounces (oz) = 226.796 grams (g)

1 ounce (oz) = 28.3495 grams (g)
"An eighth" or "an eighth of an ounce (oz)" = 3.543 grams (g)
"A quarter" or "a quarter of an ounce" = 7.087 grams (g)
"A half" or "a half of an ounce" = 14.174 grams (g)

1 kilogram (kg) = 2.204 pounds (lb)
1 kilogram (kg) = 1000 grams (g)

I AM A

NUG

YOU ARE A NUG

RAD CAT PRESS

ABOUT THE AUTHOR

Sage Liskey is an author, poet, workshop presenter, mental health advocate, and philosopher. He founded the Rad Cat Press in 2010 and is based out of Oregon. The Rad Cat Press is devoted to creating life-changing and accessible publications for the modern world.

You can like us on Facebook at www.facebook.com/radcatpress or visit www.sageliskey.com to check out other projects and free downloads also by Sage Liskey and the Rad Cat Press:

- YOU ARE A GREAT AND POWERFUL WIZARD
- The Happiest Choice: Essential Tools for Everyone's Brain Feelings
- The Happiest Choice: Condensed Edition
- A Century of Moon Phases
- Wine and Poetry Night Year One
- A Sustainability Guide for Everyday Folk
- Community How To
- The Truthagandist Primer: Effective Information Distribution for Activists
- That Was Zen, This Is Sudoku!
- Surviving the Collapse of Society: Skills to Know and Careers to Pursue

CPSIA information can be obtained
at www.ICGtesting.com
Printed in the USA
LVHW052159270121
677513LV00011B/696